WATER IN OCEANS

Isaac Nadeau

The Rosen Publishing Group's
PowerKids Press™

New York

To Joman, Becky, and the Little One

Published in 2003 by The Rosen Publishing Group, Inc.
29 East 21st Street, New York, NY 10010

First Edition

Editor: Gillian Houghton
Book Design: Maria E. Melendez

Photo Credits: Cover, title page, pp. 15, 16, 19 (bottom left and right), all page borders © CORBIS; pp. 4, 7 (map), 8, 11, 12, 15 (wave model), 16 (map), 19 (erosion model) illustrations by Maria E. Melendez; pp. 7 (top right), 12 (Earths) © Photodisc; p. 20 (Krill) © Rick Price/CORBIS; p. 20 © Digital Stock CD.

Nadeau, Isaac.
Water in oceans / Isaac Nadeau.
    p. cm. — (The water cycle)
Includes bibliographical references and index.
ISBN 0-8239-6267-9 (lib. bdg.)
1. Ocean—Juvenile literature. [1. Ocean.] I. Title.
GC21.5 .N36 2003
  551.46—dc21

                            2001006668

Manufactured in the United States of America

CONTENTS

cloud

ocean

river

Water is always in motion. It flows in rivers, floats in clouds, and moves in waves on the ocean's surface.

ALWAYS ON THE GO

Of all the amazing kinds of matter on Earth, only water is commonly found as a solid, a liquid, and a gas. Water can take on each of these states, or forms, as it moves from one place to another. Water is always on the go. Water frozen 1 mile (1.6 km) deep inside the ice sheet in Antarctica moves very slowly. Water falling from the cliffs at Niagara Falls moves fast. In the sky, **water vapor** drifts over our heads in the form of clouds and eventually will fall to the ground as rain, snow, or hail. Water moves deep under ground, filling the cracks in rocks and soil. Water even moves inside the bodies of animals and plants. This movement of water from place to place is called the water cycle. All of the water on Earth eventually makes its way back to the ocean. The world's oceans are by far the largest collections of water in the water cycle.

A WORLD OF WATER

*O*ceans are the huge bodies of salt water that surround all the islands and the continents on Earth. Although the oceans are connected, we often divide them into four major bodies of water. The Pacific Ocean is 12,500 miles (20,117 km) wide at its widest point and up to 7 miles (11 km) deep. The Atlantic Ocean is the second-largest ocean and is about half the size of the Pacific. The Indian Ocean is 4,000 miles (6,437 km) wide. The Arctic Ocean is the smallest, shallowest, and coldest of the oceans. It is far to the north and is mostly covered in ice all year. Some scientists consider the Southern Ocean, or Antarctic Ocean, to be a fifth ocean. Others divide this ocean among the southern reaches of the Pacific, Indian, and Atlantic Oceans. The Southern Ocean surrounds the frozen continent of Antarctica.

When the first photographs of Earth were taken from space, people were amazed at how blue the planet appeared. Beneath the swirling clouds, the oceans make Earth look like a blue jewel floating in space (right).

Arctic Ocean

Atlantic Ocean

Pacific Ocean

Indian Ocean

Southern Ocean, or Antarctic Ocean

Earth's oceans are often divided into the Arctic, Pacific, Atlantic, Indian, and Southern, or Antarctic, oceans (above). These oceans cover 71 percent of Earth's surface and make up 97 percent of all the water on Earth. There is more than ten times as much water in oceans as there is under ground, in the air, in lakes and rivers, and in glaciers combined!

subtropical zone

equator

WHERE THE RAIN COMES FROM

Almost all the water in the **atmosphere** comes directly from the oceans through the process of **evaporation**. About 90 percent of this water returns to the ocean as rain. The rest falls on land as rain, snow, or hail. Conditions such as wind and the warming caused by sunlight increase evaporation. In oceans the most evaporation occurs in the **subtropical** regions, directly to the north and the south of the **equator**. The subtropical regions receive a lot of sunlight. They also are almost always windy. As heat from the Sun draws water into the air, wind blows it away, causing the air to dry out. Dry air is like a sponge, sucking up more water vapor from the ocean's surface. The winds help to carry water vapor to land, where it falls as **precipitation**.

Many storms form over warm, windy subtropical waters (inset). When ocean water evaporates, it forms clouds. As the wind blows the clouds toward shore, the clouds meet the cool air over land. The water vapor becomes a liquid again and falls to Earth as rain, as in this picture.

OCEAN CURRENTS

Water is constantly moving throughout the oceans in patterns called currents. There are two main types of ocean currents. These are wind-driven currents and deep-ocean currents. Wind-driven, or surface, currents follow the patterns of the **prevailing**, or major, winds. As wind moves across the surface of an ocean, it pushes the water in the same direction. The prevailing winds cause the ocean's surface waters to move in great circles that stretch the width of the ocean. These circular currents are called **gyres**.

Deep-ocean currents occur miles (km) below the surface. These currents are driven by differences in the **density**, or heaviness, of the ocean water. The density of ocean water depends on its temperature and **salinity**, or how much salt it holds. Colder, saltier water is heavier than warmer, less salty water. The cold water sinks and the warm water rises. This sinking causes deep-ocean currents to move. Together surface and deep-ocean currents are an important part of the water cycle. They help to move the water from one place to another in the oceans.

Many wind-driven currents, as shown above, move ocean water very quickly. These gyres can carry floating objects over thousands of miles (km) of ocean water in several weeks or months. Deep-ocean currents move very slowly. Water in a deep-ocean current might not rise to the surface for 1,000 years.

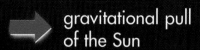 gravitational pull of the Sun

 gravitational pull of the Moon

SPRING TIDE
full Moon

NEAP TIDE
quarter phases of the Moon

SPRING TIDE
new Moon

When the Sun and the Moon are in line with Earth, the gravitational pulls of the Sun and the Moon work together, creating the highest tides (left and below right). These high tides, called spring tides, occur twice a month, during the new moon and during the full moon. The lowest tides, called neap tides, occur when the pull of the Sun and the pull of the Moon are at right angles to each other. The force of the Sun's gravity balances out the force of the Moon's gravity, causing smaller bulges (below left).

TIDES

If you were to sit on a beach by the ocean, you would notice that, over a period of several hours, the water level creeps up the beach and then slips slowly back down. These rises and falls of the ocean's surface are called tides. Tides are caused mostly by the pull of the Moon's **gravity**. As the Moon circles Earth, the Moon's gravity pulls the water toward it. Water gathers on the side of Earth closest to the Moon. On the opposite side, the pull of the Moon's gravity is weakest. However, a second high tide forms there because of the force of Earth's spinning. As the Moon travels around Earth, these collections of water move like huge waves, or swells of water. A high tide occurs as one of these two swells passes by an area. Most places have two high tides and two low tides each day.

WAVES

Most waves are caused by the wind blowing over the surface of an ocean. Waves begin as tiny ripples. As the ripples grow, the wind catches them more easily, causing them to grow larger. The size of a wave depends on how hard the wind is blowing, how long it blows, and the size of the area over which it blows. Hurricanes are large storms that begin in warm ocean waters with high-speed winds. These storms produce wind-powered waves more than 50 feet (15 m) high. Another type of wave, called a **tsunami**, is caused by earthquakes or volcanoes on the ocean floor. The power of the earthquake or the volcano causes the water above it to move away from the center of the event in huge waves at great speeds.

You can send waves along a length of rope by holding one end and shaking it. The waves move away from you, along the rope, but the rope itself does not move away from you. This is similar to how ocean waves move. Waves pass quickly over the surface of the ocean, but the water itself moves much more slowly until it breaks, or crashes, on the shore (right). Huge waves called tsunamis can be 100 miles (161 km) long and can travel 450 miles per hour (724 km/h) away from the center of an underwater event (inset). By the time it reaches the shore, a tsunami can be more than 100 feet (30 m) high and can cause a great deal of damage to buildings.

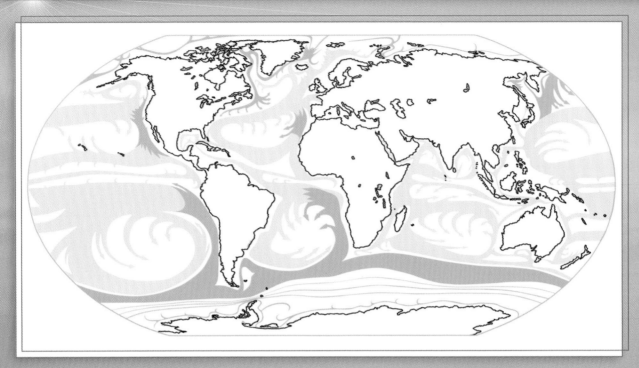

○ cold current   ○ warm current

Warm water currents, such as the Gulf Stream and the North Pacific Current, carry warm water from tropical and subtropical areas to cooler climates. Cold water currents, such as the East Greenland and Labrador currents, carry cold water south from the Arctic Circle and north from the Antarctic Ocean.

OCEANS AND CLIMATE

The oceans play a big role in Earth's weather. Ocean waters are slower to warm and to cool than is the surrounding land. For this reason, coastal areas generally have milder temperatures than do areas farther inland. Gyres often bring tropical air and water from the equator to the north and the south. The Gulf Stream, a surface current that moves across the Atlantic Ocean north of the equator, carries warm air and water from the Gulf of Mexico to New York and across the Atlantic Ocean to England. On a global scale, the oceans help to keep the climate suitable for living things. The oceans cover most of Earth's surface, so they receive most of the sunlight that comes to Earth. Much of the sunlight is reflected back into the atmosphere. The sunlight **absorbed** by the oceans helps to keep Earth at a fairly constant temperature.

WHERE THE OCEAN MEETS THE LAND

The coast is constantly **eroded** by crashing waves. Over time these waves can cause cliff walls to crumble. The rocks and boulders of the broken cliff face continue to erode as waves smash them into one another and scrape them with sand. Eventually these boulders become sand, too. As the water moves in and out, much of the sand is left behind, forming beaches. Beaches also form in areas such as **bays**, where land extends into the ocean and protects the shore from heavy waves. Because there are fewer waves, more sand is tossed ashore than is washed away. Sand also is carried by rivers. At the mouths, where the rivers empty into the oceans, sand collects to form beaches. Pebbles and skeletons of tiny animals are also found on beaches.

18

cliff

beach

bay

river

sand
dune

sandbar

A variety of natural features form on ocean coasts. Dunes are formed by sand blown by the wind. Sandbars and beaches are collections of tiny pieces of eroded rock and material released by nearby rivers and streams as they empty into the ocean. Bottom, left and right: Large, jagged cliffs are created as waves crash against the land.

The ocean is an important part of the water cycle, but it is also an important part of the life cycle. There is life everywhere in the ocean, from tiny krill and sea horses to huge animals such as whales. These animals rely on the water cycle to bring them nutrients. Humans and other land animals rely on many of these animals as a source of food.

LIFE IN THE OCEANS

*L*ife can be found throughout the ocean, from the surface to the floor and from the open ocean to the shore. Close to the shore, rivers wash **nutrients** from the land into the ocean. The shallow waters allow sunlight to reach all the way to the ocean floor. Underwater plants draw energy, or power, from the Sun to make food. These plants are eaten by many animals in the ocean, which in turn are eaten by other animals. Even far from shore, life exists. **Plankton** are **microscopic** plants and animals floating in the waves and just beneath the water's surface. Many animals, including krill, eat plankton. Krill are tiny shrimp that swim in large schools. Blue whales, the largest animals in the world, suck up the krill in great mouthfuls. As do living things on land, all living things in the ocean need to take water into their bodies to stay alive.

*E*ach day millions of people earn a living from the oceans. Billions of pounds (kg) of saltwater fish are caught for food each year. Huge ships carry food, cars, oil, and other **cargo** across the oceans. Important **minerals** are taken from ocean waters for use in medicines. In some places, the energy of the waves is used to produce electricity. Oil and natural gas are taken from beneath the ocean floor.

People have a big effect on the oceans' resources. In many places, the numbers of fish are growing smaller because people are catching too many too fast. Ships carrying oil can become damaged and spill their cargoes, harming the living things in the ocean. Around the world, people are learning that it is important for us to take care of the oceans so that they can continue to take care of us.

GLOSSARY

absorbed (uhb-ZORBD) Taken in.

atmosphere (AT-muh-sfeer) The layer of air that surrounds Earth.

bays (BAYZ) Inlets formed along the shore by land that extends into the ocean, protecting the shore from the heaviest waves.

cargo (KAR-goh) The goods carried by a ship, an aircraft, or another vehicle.

density (DEN-sih-tee) A measure of how tightly together a material is packed.

eroded (ih-ROHD-id) Worn away over time.

equator (ih-KWAY-tur) An imaginary line around Earth that separates it into two parts, northern and southern.

evaporation (ih-va-puh-RAY-shun) When a liquid changes into a gas.

gravity (GRA-vih-tee) The natural force that causes objects to move or tend to move toward the center of Earth.

gyres (JYRZ) Circular currents on the ocean's surface.

microscopic (my-kroh-SKAH-pik) So small it can only be seen with a microscope.

minerals (MIN-rulz) Natural ingredients from Earth's soil, such as coal or copper, that come from the ground and are not plants, animals, or other living things.

nutrients (NOO-tree-ints) Anything that a living thing needs to live and grow.

plankton (PLANK-ten) Plants and animals that drift with water currents.

precipitation (preh-sih-pih-TAY-shun) Any moisture that falls from the sky.

prevailing (prih-VAYL-ing) Most common or strongest.

salinity (suh-LIH-neh-tee) The amount of salt in something.

subtropical (sub-TRAH-pih-kuhl) Having to do with the warm parts of Earth to the north and south of the equator.

tsunami (soo-NAH-mee) A huge wave created by an underwater earthquake or volcano.

water vapor (WAH-tuhr VAY-pur) Water in its gaseous state.

INDEX

WEB SITES

Due to the changing nature of Internet links, PowerKids Press has developed an online list of Web sites related to the subject of this book. This site is updated regularly. Please use this link to access the list:

www.powerkidslinks.com/wc/ocean/